THE QUOTABLE RONALD REAGAN

The Common Sense and Straight Talk
of Former California Governor
Ronald Reagan

Edited and Compiled by Joseph R. Holmes

Copies of the Quotable Ronald Reagan are available in bulk quantities of 25 or more at discount prices.

For information write:

> JRH & Associates, Inc.
> 3702 Fourth Ave., Suite C
> San Diego, CA 92103

or Telephone:
> (714) 298-1383

INTRODUCTION

For several years, I was associated with Ronald Reagan, then Governor of California, as the producer of a weekly television program called "Governor and Students."

The program brought together Reagan and students from all over California in unrehearsed "rap" sessions where the youngsters would ask the Governor any questions on their minds. The video taped sessions were then distributed, without any editing, on a State network of public broadcast and cable systems all over California so that young people and others who watched would have a better understanding of government.

During those many, many hours when Governor Reagan was on the receiving end of very direct questions on every conceivable subject from these high school students, I came to two conclusions:

One, that these young people asked far more penetrating and interesting questions than the regular press corps that slithered around the Governor's heels, and two, Ronald Reagan was one hell of a man.

He never asked me to edit out one question or answer during the more than fifty hours of television rap sessions we did together. He thoroughly enjoyed the give and take discussions with these young people and never tried to talk down to them. As a matter of fact, he respected their opinions and appeared to receive as much from the meeting as the youngsters.

It is a matter of dismay to me today to hear of the misconceptions surrounding this man I believe history will judge as California's finest Governor.

When he became Governor on an unpleasant, chilly night in January of 1967, the State was in a terrible mess. California government was spending one million dollars more than it was taking in every day. When he left office in January, 1975, the budget he left for the incoming Governor was balanced and showed a surplus of 200 million dollars.

In January of 1967, State employee rolls were increasing at a rate of better than seven per cent each year. When Ronald Reagan left office eight years later, the total for the entire eight years was an increase of only two per cent in State employees.

In January of 1967, welfare rolls were increasing in the State of California at the rate of more than 40,000 persons each month. When Governor Reagan left office eight years later, that growth had stopped and welfare rolls had been reduced by over 350,000 persons. Without Reagan reform, welfare would have cost California taxpayers at least one billion dollars more.

The accomplishments of the Reagan administration will take a book in themselves, but I will touch on one other area which we found frequently was a hot subject during the television question and answer sessions.

That subject was California education and, perhaps, on this question was the greatest amount of misinformation spread to young people by the California news media.

Talk to most any college student or even high school senior in California and he or she will tell you that the Reagan administration viciously cut funds from the state college and university budgets. The fact is: He did not.

During the eight years of the Reagan Administration, funds for the State colleges were increased from $167 million to $480 million annually, an increase of 163 per cent, while enrollment increased 78 per cent. The University of California system budget increased under Reagan from $240 million to $493 million, up 105 per cent, while enrollment increased 43 per cent.

State student scholarships and loans increased from $4.7 million to $43 million under Ronald Reagan, an increase of 914 per cent.

Those facts are readily available to any student of government, in or out of school.

Of course, there is much more to Ronald Reagan than simply being a tremendous administrator who led California from the brink of fiscal and moral bankruptcy to solvency in eight years. There is the man with a delightful sense of humor and with a remarkable ability to laugh at himself, a trait not usually found in those who are constantly immersed in the roar of the crowd as public figures. These are two of my favorite true stories about his ability to not take himself too seriously:

It was during one of the National Governors Conferences in New York and Governor Ronald Reagan was arriving back at his hotel one afternoon after a series of morning meetings with his fellow governors.

The Governor stepped out of his car at the hotel entrance into a pool of people waiting for taxis or their own cars and found himself directly in the path of a well dressed matron.

She looked and then gasped, "I know you. You're . . . You're . . . You're . . . that famous movie star . . . Ronald Coleman!"

The Governor smiled and stopped as the woman gushed how she had enjoyed his many motion pictures. Ronald Reagan thanked her and began moving toward the lobby, but the woman said, "Please, Mr. Coleman, may I have your autograph?", as she frantically searched her purse for appropriate paper and pen.

So Ronald Reagan stopped and signed, "With best wishes, Ronald Coleman." The matron went happily on her way, Reagan strode sedately through the lobby into the elevator and chuckled all the way to the seventeenth floor.

The other incident occurred some months later in California.

Rudy Garcia was the assistant press secretary to Governor Ronald Reagan. His specific assignment was to travel with the Governor on his countless stops throughout the State and nation and coordinate the requests of the news media. Wherever Ronald Reagan travels he is news. Newsmen want to talk with him, television cameramen want to film him. Garcia had to sort out the requests and set up the Governor's availability to the media on his normally brief stops.

On one of their frequent visits to San Francisco, a town whose press is not exactly favorable to Ronald Reagan, the Governor had made an early morning talk at one of the hotels and was being pursued by a mass of press when he suddenly disappeared.

Garcia became the target of the press distemper as reporters demanded to know where the Governor had gone. Finally, getting them reasonably muted so he could speak, Garcia exasperatedly announced the Governor was in the men's room and then he cracked, "See, that proves Reagan is human."

The crack found its way into the daily newspaper column of decaying San Francisco columnist Herb Caen and Garcia thought he was in hot water with the Governor. To the contrary, Reagan thought it was a great line! But he pointed out he didn't think it was of momentous importance to announce to the press each time he went to the men's room.

The following pages are the results of my listening to dozens and dozens of hours of audio tapes from the Governor and Students television series and from reading through hundreds of his speeches.

They will allow you to evaluate Ronald Reagan and what he believes in from his own words.

. . .

I sincerely hope this book of Ronald Reagan's common sense approach to Government and life will give Americans a better understanding of this man whom destiny touched and apparently will not leave alone.

Joseph R. Holmes
June 1, 1975

The Quotable
Ronald Reagan

ABILITY

This is a society where everyone can rise as high
and as far as his own ability will take him.

Students
June 21, 1973

ABORTION

I think one of the hardest decisions that I ever
had to make had to do with the abortion legisla-
tion because it was a subject I've never given
any thought to before. Suddenly I was con-
fronted by a Legislature with a bill which they
said they would amend to whatever was accept-
able to me. For the first time I had to really face
this subject and figure out morally what did I
believe was right or wrong.

Students
March 8, 1973

ADVENTURE

We must never lose that sense of adventure, that thirst for knowledge—or the determination to explore the outer limits of our own abilities.

Speech
May 18, 1973
Riverside, Calif.

ADVICE

I know that old people are always supposed to give advice, so I'll prove I'm old and give you some . . . Today with all the flood of misinformation that comes your way, be careful. Even the figures I've given you here, don't take my word for it. Check it out. Look them up. They are always in public record. But don't become a sucker generation; don't just take someone's viewpoint on what things are.

Students
May 5, 1973

AFFLUENCE

Our affluence is based on the sweat and toil of our people.

Speech
Dec. 14, 1974

AFFLUENCE

In the long post-war years of affluence, perhaps we have forgotten the simple fact that no one gave America the world's highest standard of living. We earned it, by being the most productive and efficient industrial nation in the world.

Speech,
Feb. 15, 1972

AGRICULTURE

When government uses its coercive power to intervene in the free market place, agriculture can discover it has something worse to contend with than the corn bore or the boll weevil.

Speech
Dec. 11, 1972

ALARMS

You may be weary of me sounding the same alarms. You might think, well, we have heard all this before, but somehow we muddled through. Well, that is like the window-washer who fell from the Empire State Building. When he passed the 20th floor, he said, "so far, so good."

Speech
Oct. 29, 1972

AMERICAN PEOPLE

The problems we face are problems that affect all our people. And all our people have both the right and the obligation to help solve them. Unless people control government, the government will control them.

Speech
Aug 6, 1973

AMERICAN PEOPLE

We are the showcase of the future. And it is within our power to mold that future—this year and for decades to come. It can be as grand and as great as we make it.
No crisis is beyond the capacity of our people to solve; no challenge too great.

Speech
Jan. 5, 1974

AMNESTY

I am opposed to giving draft dodgers amnesty.
Now, I will qualify that statement and say that
in all our history those men who believe that
they have made a mistake . . . those men who
are willing to face up to it and come back and
throw themselves on the mercy of our system
and our courts and say "all right I did this. I was
wrong but I want to rectify it and pay my price
to society" . . . then I think justice should be
tempered with compassion.

Students
April 26, 1973

ARROGANCE

In our nation today, government has grown too
big, too complex,—and possessed of what
Cicero called the "arrogance of officialdom."
Remote from the wishes of the people, it forgets
that ours is a system of government by the con-
sent of the governed—not the other way
around.

Speech
Sept. 7, 1973

ASPIRATIONS

Those nations and states which have secured man's highest aspirations for freedom, opportunity and justice, have always been those willing to trust their people, confident that their skills and their talents are equal to any challenge.

Speech
Jan 5, 1974

ATTITUDE

One legislator accused me of having a 19th century attitude on law and order. That is a totally false charge. I have an 18th century attitude. That is when the Founding Fathers made it clear that the safety of law abiding citizens should be one of government's primary concerns.

Speech
Sept. 7, 1973

The Quotable
Ronald Reagan

BUREAUCRATS

If a bureaucrat had been writing the 10 Commandments, a simple rock slab would not have been near enough room.

Those simple rules would have read: "Thou Shalt Not, unless you feel strongly to the contrary, or for the following stated exceptions, see paragraphs 1-10 subsection #A.

Speech
June 6, 1974

BUREAUCRATS

One of the things that is wrong with government is this idea that there is a certain group of people who will make a professional career out of government. That's fine but we also must always have an influx into government of people . . . citizens who say, "I owe the community something and therefore I will give one year, two years, three years, four or five years . . . a period out of my life to serve my community and bring to government the thinking of the man on the street, the people out here who sometimes say "why is government doing this?"

Students
March 8, 1973

BUSINESS

Private business and industry is the most over-regulated, over-taxed and under-appreciated part of America's society.

Speech
Oct. 15,1974

BUSINESS

For almost four decades, government in America has grown increasingly hostile to the business and industrial community.

Speech
Feb. 15, 1972

BUSINESS & LABOR

Labor sets its own goals, often without regard to the inflationary and even destructive impact those goals may have on other Americans. Businessmen react by raising prices because they must meet the demands of labor—even if doing so means surrendering more and more of their markets to lower priced foreign competition.

Speech
Feb. 15, 1972

The Quotable
Ronald Reagan

CAPACITY

I believe we have the talent and the capacity to solve whatever problems we face, in the cities of the states. If we can land a man on the moon, develop space ships that can travel to other planets, getting people to the shopping center or between cities swiftly, safely and conveniently is certainly not an impossible dream.

Speech
June 25, 1973

CAMPAIGNS

If you have someone who is going to put his hand in the cookie jar, he's going to do that whether there's a limit on campaign contributions or not.

Interview
Sept. 15, 1973

CAPITALISM

There was a student in North Carolina state who signed up for and then cancelled a course in history when he bought the assigned textbook, the title of which was Up Against the American Myth. The first line of the textbook read, "Capitalism stinks; we can solve the social problems by doing away with capitalism and the institutions that support it." When the professor was asked if he intended to assign another text that defended capitalism, he looked blank and said he knew of no such text.

Speech
Jan. 9, 1972

CAPITAL PUNISHMENT

I don't believe those who voted to re-establish capital punishment did so out of any feelings of vengeance or because they were blood thirsty zealots. They simply believe that criminals who murder innocent women and children, who gun down police and engage in political assassination will not be deterred by anything less than the ultimate penalty —and they are right.

For too many years, we have had a moratorium on capital punishment—unfortunately it has not been a total moratorium. Last year alone, there were 1,789 executions in California. Those who were sentenced to death had no trial by jury; no judge pronounced sentence nor were they afforded the protection of the appeal process in our legal system.

They were picked at random by their executioners, who had also appointed themselves judge and jury.

The executions took place on our streets, in the victims' homes and in places of business. If there were pleas for clemency, they went unheeded: 1,789 innocent people in our state were executed with no recognition of their constitutional rights or of the moratorium that only gave shelter to their executioners.

Speech
Sept. 7, 1973

CAPITAL PUNISHMENT

The worst moment I've ever had as Governor was in regard to an execution early in my administration, the last one held in California. The Governor does have the right to commute a sentence to life imprisonment, and I felt on reviewing all of the evidence, that I couldn't do that. This case had been appealed all the way up to the United States Supreme Court.

Every court, every legal process upheld the rightness of that death sentence, and I had to agree with them. But I think it is the worst moment any man has, because you can't help wonder in your mind . . . should you or shouldn't you do this, as the moment approaches.

Students
March 8, 1973

CAPITAL PUNISHMENT

. . . There were people who were opposed to the death penalty who came to the Capitol. As a matter of fact, one group of people held a service on the Capitol steps and then they asked that all the church bells of the State be tolled at the moment of an execution. I had no quarrel with that and I told them that I didn't. I said that I think that any of us would want to be praying for the soul of another human being in a moment like that but I said I thought it might also be appropriate to toll the church bells every time someone was murdered in California.

Students
March 8, 1973

CAPITAL PUNISHMENT

Whenever one speaks of capital punishment, there is a danger of being cast as a zealot, waving the bloody shirt. And I am fully aware that many citizens honestly oppose capital punishment on moral grounds or because of their own compassionate views. I respect their opinions. They are entitled to express them and to seek to convince others of the validity of their belief.

But a majority of our citizens strongly believe that capital punishment *is* a deterrent to crime. And I cannot help but draw some degree of significance from the fact that during the time we have had an almost total moritorium on capital punishment, the rate of violent crime has escalated steadily.

Speech
Aug. 1, 1973

CHALLENGE

The fundamental challenge facing America today is simply the restoration of America's financial stability in a world economy dangerously out of kilter because of inflation.

Speech
Oct. 15, 1974

CHARITY

We have a kind of generosity that is rather unusual in the whole world because from the beginning we've accepted the responsibility of voluntary giving for great causes. The more you transfer this to the state, the more you get to be like so many of the older countries where people say "its not my responsibility, there's somebody in government who is supposed to do that."

Well today, in this country, we give 21 and one-half billion dollars voluntary to charitable and educational institutions and so forth.

Interview
May 8, 1973

CHICAGO

It is a homecoming for me and I could be very nostalgic. Of course when I lived here before, I was a Democrat and my whole family were Democrats. As a matter of fact, I had an uncle who lived here in Chicago who won a medal once for never having missed voting in an election for 15 years . . . and he had been dead for fourteen.

Speech
August 9, 1973

COLLEGES

The very existence of the independent college and university helps to assure and safeguard academic freedom for both students and faculty. This competition, the fact that you are still in business, gives the educational consumer (the student) a greater variety of choice, not only to meet his academic goals, but also to nurture and provide for the spiritual experience that is part of any complete educational program.

Speech
April 30, 1973

COMFORT

An air-conditioned car or home may be a luxury to someone who lives in a colder climate. But it is not a luxury to someone who must live and work in a desert climate.

Speech
Nov. 17, 1972

COMMON SENSE

Government can be brought under control if enough people are willing to stand the gaff and take the heat, and fight for common sense solutions.

Speech
Oct. 15, 1974

COMMUNICATIONS

"Communications is not only somebody talking but somebody being willing to listen."

Speech
June 10, 1973

COMMUNISM

I have had students sometimes ask me if there is really such a great difference between our two systems. They say they have read the Soviet constitution and their laws, and found frequent use of the words freedom and justice.

The right of free speech, which we often take for granted, is mentioned too. But there is a difference between our two constitutions. The difference is so subtle we often do overlook it, but it is so great it tells the entire story. Their constitution says government grants these rights. Our constitution says we, the people, are born with these rights and no government can take them from us.

Speech
May 2, 1974

COMPETITION

There can be no prosperity or even freedom for our people if we ever abandon the competitive economic system that transferred this country into the strongest nation in the world.

Speech
Dec. 11, 1972

CONSERVATIVES

I think the so-called conservative is today, what was in the classic sense, the liberal. The classical liberal, during the Revolutionary time, was a man who wanted less power for the King and more power for the people. He wanted people to have more say in the running of their lives and he wanted protection for the God given right of the people. He did not believe those rights were dispensations granted by the King to the people, he believed that he was born with them. Well, that today is the conservative.

Interview
Sept. 15, 1973

CONSTITUTION

Our constitution is a document that protects the people from government.

Students
Sept. 17, 1973

COURAGE

When some of our ancestors were crossing the plains in their Conestoga wagons, braving the elements, risking disease, starvation and death in the wilderness, they had a blunt saying that symbolized their determination.

In the great move West, they said: "The cowards never started and the weak died on the way."

Throughout man's history, there have always been doubters and cynics, people who said it cannot be done and did not want anyone to try.

But the history of our civilization, the great advances that made it possible, is not a story of cynics or doomcriers. It is a gallant chronicle of the optimists, the determined people, men and women who dreamed great dreams and dared to try whatever it takes to make them come true.

Speech
May 18, 1973

COURTS

I sometimes think if someone appealed the Ten Commandments to some of our courts, they would rule—"Thou shalt not, unless you feel strongly to the contrary."

Speech
June 22, 1973

CREDIT

I have a little bronze plaque on my desk and I hope I can live by the inscription it bears—"You can accomplish much if you don't care who gets the credit."

Speech
June 28, 1972

CRIME RATE

I believe the experience of the past eight years has demonstrated that there is a cause and effect relationship in the crime rate. When we passed a tougher law on drunk driving, the number of arrests went up, and the number of traffic deaths caused by drunk driving went down.

Speech
Dec. 4, 1974

CRIME

The problem of crime is not an abstraction to be debated in some academic tearoom. It is a daily threat to the lives and safety of our people.

Speech
Feb. 11, 1974

CRIME

The crime problem has indeed become a matter of widespread concern, even among people of different philosophies. Today's hardliner on law and order is yesterday's liberal who was mugged last night.

Speech
Aug. 1, 1973

CRIME

Court rulings stacked almost entirely on the side of the law breaker, a lack of uniform sentencing patterns for identical crimes, an over reliance on probation and perhaps, a too optimistic view that hardened criminals can be easily rehabilitated; all those things add up to a seeming inability, a failure of the criminal justice system to fulfill its basic purpose. To most of our people, the purpose of the law and the criminal justice system is clear and simple: it is to protect the innocent and bring the guilty to justice.

This does not mean that we have no regard for the Constitutional rights we are all sworn to protect. Safeguarding the rights of the accused is and must always be a legitimate and critical part of the judicial system.

Speech
Aug 1, 1973

CRIME

Murder is murder, whether it is committed as an individual act or a protest against society.

Speech
May 2, 1974

CRIME

When a law breaker can kill without facing the prospect of the ultimate penalty, when most convicted criminals know that they probably will not wind up in prison, we cannot say we have effective deterrents to even more criminal activity.

Speech
Aug. 1. 1973

CRIME

We will not reduce crime by legalizing a lot of things that have always been against the law. All the rules and efficient court procedures will not assure justice unless our people, a massive majority of them, are willing to accept the rule of law as a necessary alternative to the rule of the mob.

Speech
Oct. 29, 1972

CURES

When government decides to solve something, we have learned to be wary. The cure may not always be worse than the disease, but it is usually bigger and it costs more.

Speech
Oct. 29, 1972

The Quotable
Ronald Reagan

DEFICITS

When an individual or a business has a lean year, they have to prune expenses and work for better days. When government has a deficit, it expects to solve that deficit by handing you a higher tax bill.

Speech
Aug. 6, 1973

DEFICIT FINANCING

Continual deficit financing, year in and year out, is not the path to prosperity. It is the road to national bankruptcy. It is like a self-fulfilling prophecy because the more the government goes into debt, the more it must borrow.

Speech
Nov. 14, 1974

DEMOCRATS

We believe the best way to assure prosperity is to generate more jobs. The Democrats believe in more welfare.

Speech
Nov. 15, 1973

DEMOCRATS

The democratic party has gone more and more in a belief in centralized authority; they believe that the problems are too big for states and local governments. They also believe in the Galbreath theory of economics which is that the government should take more money in taxes because the government can do a better job of spending money on the people's behalf than the people can.

Students
June 18, 1973

DEMOCRATS

They sponsored a war on poverty. And six years later, there were more people on welfare than ever before. They spoke piously and loudly of peace, but the policies they followed perpetuated the longest war in our history.

Speech
June 22, 1972

DEMOCRATS

We believe government should be more efficient. They believe in more government, period.

Speech
Nov. 5, 1973

DEMOCRATS

We believe our people are paying too much of their income in taxes now and that government should do everything it can to reduce that intolerable burden. Our opponents advocate solutions that will mean higher taxes and more and more big brother control over the lives of our people.

Speech
Nov. 15, 1973

DOLLAR

Do you remember back in the days when you thought that nothing could replace the dollar. Today it practically has!

Speech
August 9, 1973

DREAMS

There is no question that we have failed to live up to the dreams of the founding fathers many times and in many places. Sometimes we do better than others. But all in all, the one thing that we must be on guard against is thinking that because of this, the system has failed. The system has not failed. Some human beings have failed the system.

Students
June 21, 1973

DRUGS

The best hope of saving young people from drug addiction is from education.

Speech
Oct. 29, 1972

DRUGS

A whole generation of young people has been exposed to the drug fads and the drug culture. And too many have been lured into accepting the idea that drug addiction is somehow an expression of personal freedom.

Speech
May 2, 1974

DRUGS

Hundreds of thousands of our young people have become hooked by narcotics, lured into tragedy and a life of shame by the Pied Pipers of the so-called drug culture.

Speech
Feb. 11, 1974

The Quotable
Ronald Reagan

ECOLOGISTS

There used to be an expression—"Stop the world, I want to get off"—now it is a movement; they want to stop the world and put us off."

Speech
Nov. 12, 1972

ECONOMICS

During the build-up for the war in Southeast Asia, America's economic position became disturbed. Our country drifted into that conflict without a definite plan for victory or for dealing with the inflation that inevitably accompanies war.

Speech
Oct. 12, 1972

ECONOMICS

Someone once said the most satisfying thing in life is to park on what is left of the other fellow's nickel. That is a clever wisecrack, but it is bad economics. Sooner or later, the free time on the parking meter runs out.

Speech
Dec. 14, 1974

EDUCATION

What I support is an idea of not only a tax credit for part of your tuition, but a tax credit up to a certain limit for a contribution to those schools which are privately supported. For example, you could compute your income tax and if you owed $1,000 you could take $100 and instead of sending it to the government you could send it to the school of your choice.

Students
April 12, 1973

EDUCATION

I believe in local control of education and the legislature has mandated too many programs on local education. In order to get money, the legislature has said to each school district, "you have to spend every dollar exactly as we tell you." This in itself is backward.

Students
April 12, 1973

EDUCATION

Those who wondered about the campus disruptions might find at least a partial answer to student unrest in the polls of student opinion taken throughout that period. From beginning to end—and unfortunately, it is still true today —the grievances cited most frequently by students involved what they perceived to be faculty neglect of the student and his needs.

It was not Vietnam. It was not student power. The grievance mentioned most frequently was the student's inability to find the professor, the too common use of graduate teaching assistants in the classroom rather than the professors and faculty the students expected to find there.

Speech
April 30, 1973

EDUCATION

A century ago, his eminence Cardinal John Henry Newman observed that education is not recreation or amusement. It is hard, demanding mental discipline applied to a serious purpose.

"Do not say the people must be educated when, after all, you mean amused, refreshed, soothed, put into good spirits and good humor or kept from vicious excesses."

If the good Cardinal could have been around for the campus ferment of the 1960s, he would have found that his words still have great validity.

During that period of turmoil and unrest, there were those on campus who seemed to believe that it was a proper role of the university or college to amuse rather than to educate. And there were a lot of people off campus who did not find that amusing.

Speech
April 30, 1973

EDUCATION

If we accept the philosophy that everything is the government's obligation, then I can see all private universities and colleges disappearing and we would have a state wide and nation wide system of public educational institutions. Well, they had that in Germany when Hitler was alive, and when the government said "burn the books," the professors burned the books.

Interview
May 8, 1973

ELDERLY

It's been said that civilization is judged by how well it takes care of its young and old. I don't think that just means putting up money for the assistance of the old. There is a hell of a lot more that the old need. They need to feel needed, for one thing.

Interview
May 8, 1973

ENDANGERED SPECIES

There seems to be an organized, well-financed lobby determined to preserve the natural habitat and comfort of every species except man. Well, it is time to remember that we are ecology too.

Speech
Nov. 12, 1972

ENEMIES

We must ask ourselves if we are willing to risk all that we call the American way on the naive hope that our potential enemies have mellowed so much that they no longer have aggressive designs.

Speech
Oct. 12, 1972

ENERGY

The real energy crisis is a lack of decisive action, not next year or two or three years down the line, but *now*.

Speech
Feb. 6, 1974

ENERGY

With 6 percent of the world's population, we have been using about 35 percent of the world's energy. And if we are honest with ourselves, we know we have been wasting some of that 35 percent and can conserve some of it by doing things a little differently.

Speech
Dec. 14, 1974

ENERGY CRISIS

They say a pessimist is someone who sees a calamity in every opportunity and an optimist is a fellow who sees an opportunity in every calamity. Well, I do not believe the energy problem is a national calamity yet. It just might be an historic opportunity for our country to again demonstrate the inherent strength of our system, by accelerating the technology we must have to meet our energy needs.

Speech
Dec. 14, 1974

ENVIRONMENT

We must consider the adverse environmental impact of every major activity in our society and find reasonable, workable ways to minimize that impact, but without at the same time bringing economic development to a sudden and catastrophic halt.

Speech
April 7. 1972

ENVIRONMENT

Fifty-two percent of California is government owned land. If you build on every foot of California that is in private ownership, you would still have over half the state in its natural state because it is government owned . . . the natural forests, parks, deserts and so forth.

Students
April 12, 1973

ENVIRONMENT

We do not have to choose between the environment and jobs. We can set a common sense course between those who would cover the whole country with concrete in the name of progress and those who think you should not build a house unless it looks like a bird's nest or a rabbit hole.

Speech
April 27, 1973

ENVIRONMENTALISTS

But it seems no matter how much we do, there is still a very active fringe element in the environmental movement that never seems to be satisfied. Orderly progress in solving this very complex problem, in a way that does not paralyze the economy, is not enough.

Speech
Nov. 12, 1973

ETERNAL LIFE

Too many people, especially in government, feel that the nearest thing to eternal life we will ever see on this earth is a government program.

Speech
May 10, 1972

EXPERTISE

I have been abroad in recent months on an errand for the President. I do not pretend that having seen the monkey, I can now run the circus.

Speech
Oct. 12, 1972

The Quotable
Ronald Reagan

FARMERS

Farmers are among the strongest conservationists in this land. They earn their living from the land and they know man has to be careful with this precious resource.

Speech
April 27, 1973

FARMERS

Forty years ago, government decided to solve the problem of the farmers. Now forty years and scores of billions later, we only have a third as many farmers as when we started, but we have three times as many employees in the department of agriculture.

Speech
Oct. 29, 1972

FLEAS

Fleas are a part of the ecological cycle, but I doubt if a dog thinks he is doing something to destroy ecology by wearing a flea collar.

Speech
March 7, 1973

FISCAL COMMON SENSE

Americans have had their night on the town of social tinkering and social experimentation. They are now suffering the morning after, and they are hungry for some good old ham and eggs fiscal common sense.

Speech
Aug. 9, 1973

FEAR

When we say we want to solve the crime problem, what we really mean is that we want government to be able to guarantee every citizen that most of all freedoms; freedom from fear. Freedom from the threat of muggers and freedom to be able to walk the streets.

Speech
Dec. 4, 1974

FORESTS

We must cut trees no faster than trees are growing, to leave forests in such a way that just as a farmer always has another crop coming along, there will always be trees to cut and there will always be forests.

Rocklin School
March 8, 1973

FORESTERS LAW

Forester's Law holds that "in complicated situations, efforts to improve things often make them worse, sometimes much worse, on occasion calamitous."

Those who have seized the leadership of the Democratic Party are practitioners of Forester's Law. They complicate our problems with government solutions that never seem to work. No matter how often a program fails, they prescribe more of the same—at higher cost.

Speech
Feb. 3, 1973

FREEDOM

I have always believed that government is here to protect us from each other. Government cannot possibly set itself up to protect us from ourselves.

I happen to believe it is fine to have seat belts in your car. I thoroughly am for them, because I know how many people have been killed in minor accidents because they did not have their seat belts on. Anyone who does not wear one, particularly sitting in the front seat is foolish. But I would fight to the death any bill that says you've got to wear one because by not wearing one you are not harming someone else.

A better example is riding motorcycles. I agree with requiring that you have either got to wear a wind screen or goggles. That's because if you get hit in the eye with a bug or rock, you can come across the line and do something to me, if I am coming the other way. I also think you are foolish to ride a motorcycle without a helmet. But I would be against any law that said you had to wear a helmet. That isn't protecting anyone else. Freedom should be the right to be stupid if you want to be.

Students
Feb. 13, 1973

FREEDOM

With freedom goes responsibility, a responsibility that can only be met by the individual himself. This is an eternal truth as valid today as it was in 1791 when Edmund Burke said, "Men are qualified for civil liberty in the exact proportion to their disposition to put moral chains upon their appetites . . ."

Speech
May 2, 1974

FREEDOM

Under our system, we all are public servants. Yet, at what point does government become the dominant force in the economy? When does government become the master, instead of the servant? When government takes almost half or more than half of the people's earnings, freedom is clearly threatened.

Speech
May 16, 1973

FREEDOM

Freedom is indivisible—there is no "s" on the
end of it. You can erode freedom, diminish it,
but you cannot divide it and choose to keep
"some freedoms" while giving up others.

Speech
May 4, 1972

FREEDOM

History makes it plain that unless restrained,
government proliferates to a point where its
cost bankrupts the people at the same time it
robs them of their freedom.

Speech
Sept. 7, 1973

FREEDOM

It is time we realized that profit, property and freedom are inseparable. You can not have any one of them without the others.

Speech
Oct. 15, 1974

FREEDOM

America cannot survive in the 1970's if our people have only a half-hearted commitment to freedom.

Speech
Sept. 30, 1972

FREE ENTERPRISE

It is old-fashioned, even reactionary to remind people that free enterprise has done more to reduce poverty than all the government programs dreamed up by democracy.

Speech
May 4, 1972

FREE ENTERPRISE

What some of our people seem to have forgotten is the fact that America's prosperity was not a gift from government or anyone else. Free Enterprise, not government, is the source from which our blessings flow.

Speech
Dec. 14, 1974

FREE MARKET

The tragedy is that our inflation problems are not the fault of the free market system. We stumbled into inflation because we strayed too far away from the free market concept.

Speech
Oct. 15, 1974

FREE ENTERPRISE

I think it is time everyone in business and industry in this country recognize that for the second time in this century, business and the free enterprise system are under assault—an unremitting assault by those who would change this system quite drastically.

Speech
Nov. 10, 1972

FREEWAYS

Freeways are not monsters . . . we save human lives every time we add a mile of freeway. The freeway fatality rate is about 2.2 and on highways and streets is about 5.

Students
April 12, 1975

FREE TIME

I have to confess something to you. Before I became Governor, my television programs sort of worked down so that they didn't take many days out of the week, so I was able to spend more time farming than I was on television. It was kind of a subsidized retirement. And I loved it. I miss having a ranch. You might also be interested to know I am a very strong conservationist. We burned our own firewood in our fireplace for the past twenty years. We never cut down a tree to do it unless the tree was dead. We take limbs that the wind takes off, and so forth, I've planted more trees than have had to be taken down. Yes, I love that and when I can now, I try to get to a horse. That is my biggest love.

Students
March 22, 1973

FUTURE

If you want to know which way to go in the future, you have to know which path you took in the past and where you stepped in a gopher hole along the way.

Speech
Oct. 15, 1974

The Quotable
Ronald Reagan

GAMBLING

I would hate to see legalized gambling in California, nor do I favor a lottery. We ought to finance the state by the strength of our people and not by their weaknesses.

Students
June 21, 1973

GOLDEN RULE

With freedom goes responsibility. Sir Winston Churchill once said you can have 10,000 regulations and still not have respect for law. We might start with the Ten Commandments. If we lived by the Golden Rule, there would be no need for other laws.

Speech
Sept. 7, 1973

GOVERNMENT

Common sense practices of the private sector will work in government if you will just give them a chance.

Interview
Sept. 18, 1973

GOVERNMENT

There is nothing wrong with our system. Somebody is handling the machinery wrong.

Interview
Sept. 15, 1973

GOVERNMENT

When you start talking about government as "we" instead of "they," you have been in office too long.

Interview
Sept. 15, 1973

GOVERNOR

I have never found anything that was as challenging or as fulfilling as being Governor of California. This has been the greatest experience of my life, maybe partly because I not only get to read the script, I help write it.

Students
Sept. 29, 1973

GOVERNMENT INTERFERENCE

I think that anyone who has a business has got a right to run it the way he wants to. If he decides everybody has to wear neckties or everybody doesn't have to wear neckties, that is up to him. I just don't like to see government passing laws to force everybody to do what every government thinks they should do. I recognize in saying this that when I take Nancy and my son to dinner, I can't go to a restaurant which refuses to serve long hairs.

Students
June 18, 1973

GOVERNMENT

Prosperity is something created by people and their industries and business for which government takes credit. There are always those who insist government must keep pace with our free society by increasing in size, in cost and ultimately and inevitably in power. It will not come as a shock to you, I am sure, to hear that even though I am part of government, I disagree.

Government must keep pace with the changing needs of our state and its people to be sure that government can fulfill its legitimate obligations.

But if our people are to enjoy the real income gains they have earned, government must not create inflation or siphon their increased earnings into government coffers.

Government has an inborn tendency to grow. And, left to itself, it will grow beyond the control of the people. Only constant complaint by the people will inhibit this growth.

Speech
Aug. 6, 1973

GOVERNMENT

Heaven help us if government ever gets into the business of protecting us from ourselves.

Students
April 12, 1973

GOVERNMENT

You ought to weigh everything that's proposed by government . . . against the loss of a personal freedom.

Students
April 12, 1973

GOVERNMENT

The more government we can keep at local levels in local hands, the better off we are and the more freedom we will have.

Students
April 12, 1973

GOVERNMENT

Government in the United States at every level has been on a long financial drunk. We are in the first stages of the hangover: inflation and debasement of the dollar. And we are beset by helpful souls who would have us believe that what we need is more of what got us into this condition to begin with.

For a look at where we will be if we do not sober up in a hurry, hark back to Germany of the 1920's. Workers were given time off every two hours to spend their earnings before the value of their money dropped. Germans carried 50,000 mark notes for lunch money. And that wild inflation brought them, finally, an Adolf Hitler.

Speech
Oct. 15, 1973

GOVERNMENT

To be more responsive to the people, we must have enough government to carry out all of government's legitimate responsibilities, but not one bit more.

Speech
Sept. 7, 1973

GOVERNMENT

The tragic inescapable truth is: government does not have all the answers. In too many instances, government does not solve problems; it subsidizes them.

Speech
Nov. 14, 1974

GOVERNMENT

For too many years, government has been growing in size and power with no regard for the economic consequences. And government loves it.

Speech
Oct. 15, 1974

GOVERNMENT

Wisdom in government is not a one-way street that always runs downhill. More often, the higher up the ladder of government you go, the less common sense you find.

Speech
Oct. 24, 1973

GOVERNMENT

Government does not solve problems; it subsidizes them.

Speech
Dec. 11, 1972

GOVERNOR

There are some days you go home so frustrated that you get in the shower and you make speeches to the walls of the shower. But there are other days when you go home and feel ten feet tall because you have solved a problem.

Students
March 8, 1973

The Quotable
Ronald Reagan

HABIT

We sure can't be like the fellow's wife who used to cut off both ends of the ham before she cooked it. When he asked her why she did that, she said because that's the way her mother always did it.

One day, he got the chance to ask his mother-in-law why she cut off both ends of the ham before she cooked it. And she said because that's the way *her* mother did it.

Came the holidays and Grandma was visiting and he told her about it and asked if that was true—why did she cut off both ends of the ham before she cooked it? She said, "that's simple. I never had a pan big enough to get the whole ham in it."

Speech
May 31, 1974

HERITAGE

In recent years there have been voices raised among us that would so emphasize our heritage, where we came from, that they would separate us once again and have a nation of separatist groups based on ethnic, racial or religious lines. Don't let that happen. Up until a few years ago the great pride of this nation was that we were a melting pot. It didn't mean that we forgot our heritage, that we weren't proud, that we didn't keep alive the customs of whatever was our background.

Students
June 21, 1973

HIGHWAYS

Since 1916, the population of the United States has doubled, the number of vehicles has increased 30 times, yet highway mileage has increased less than one third. In some areas, highways require less land area than we used for horses and wagons before the automobile was invented.

Speech
Nov. 12, 1973

HIGHWAYS

There has been far too much mythology about the so-called adverse impact of highways and not enough facts about how vital our highways are to the prosperity, convenience and well-being of our people.

Speech
Nov. 17, 1972

HISTORY

Every generation has challenged the customs and values of its predecessors and there is nothing wrong with that. There is something wrong, however, with rejecting all the lessons of the past simply because they are old.

Speech
June 22, 1972

HOMEOWNER

I would like to see the homeowner taxed only on the basis of what costs actually are associated with property such as streets, sewers, police and fire protection and not welfare and education.

Students
April 12, 1973

HORSES

If we had stuck with the horse, we would have
had another pollution problem by now.

Speech
March 7, 1973

HOUSING

The whole history of government's direct in-
volvement in housing, particularly in financing,
is a history of failure—not once, or twice, but
time after time.

Speech
Nov. 14, 1974

HOUSING

The Federal government set out some years ago to build 26 million new housing units. They started all their urban development programs and bulldozed faster than they built. The result was we ended up with 250,000 fewer homes than when they started out.

Students
April 12, 1973

The Quotable
Ronald Reagan

ICC

If the Interstate Commerce Commission had been in business during the pioneer days, the 49ers would still be trying to find out what the rules are for crossing the Mississippi River.

Speech
Oct. 15, 1974

INFLATION

Inflation is like radioactivity. It is cumulative. It piles up until one day you find it out of control.

Speech
Nov. 14, 1974

INFLATION

The truth is: there is one reason for inflation in America and that is simply that government for too long has been spending too much money.

Speech
Oct. 15, 1974

INFLATION

Unless we bring inflation under control, we can never expect to deal with any of the other problems we face as a nation.

Speech
Oct. 15, 1974

INFLATION

The truth is that government is responsible for inflation. Government deliberately planned an inflation by deficit spending.

Interview
Feb. 7, 1974

INJUSTICE

When I say ours is the best and most advanced system of political freedom yet devised by man, I certainly do not mean that we are perfect. I hope none of us will ever be so smug as to think that there are no more injustices to correct, no more wrongs to right.

Speech
May 2, 1974

The Quotable
Ronald Reagan

LABOR

Roughly, labor gets about seven-eighths of the dollar that business takes in . . . the owners, investors, people who put up the money for the business, receive about one-eighth of the dollar.

Interview
Feb. 7, 1974

LAND

One of the great freedoms in this country that was unknown in most places in the world was and is the right of ownership of land. Most of the land throughout the world belonged to a royal family and could be given as a dispensation; but in this country anyone can own the place he lives in, a man's home can be his castle, this is his and he cannot be invaded without due process of law and so forth. Now, I can see that there are people so imbued with the desire to protect the environment that they would restrict and take away that right of individual ownership. What good does it do for you to hold the deed to your property if government can tell you everything you can do with that property? I think we have to be on guard against that.

Students
Sept. 17, 1973

LAW

It is no accident those civilizations which left man his greatest legacy were those which took the first steps toward formalizing a system of law.

Speech
May 2, 1974

LAW

Respect for the law . . . for the ideal of justice for all . . . for equality . . . these things must come from within society itself.

Speech
Oct. 29, 1972

LAW ENFORCEMENT

We must give law enforcement the tools it needs if our people are to enjoy again the right to live and work and play in safety.

Speech
Sept. 7, 1973

LAW

The search for truth in the courtroom is not a game of legal chess, with the rights of society cast as an unwilling pawn. Perhaps more than anything else, we need a change of attitude, from permissiveness to realism.

Speech
Feb. 11, 1974

LAW

The teaching of respect for the law cannot be left to education alone. It is a responsibility we all must assume, in our daily lives, in every school, in our churches, throughout our social structure.

Speech
May 2, 1974

LAWFUL SOCIETY

We must recognize that preserving and protecting a lawful society is a responsibility of every
citizen. The law cannot assure justice unless a
majority of our people are willing to accept the
rule of law, not because a police car is patrolling
nearby, but because it is morally right.

Speech
Sept. 7, 1973

LAWFUL SOCIETY

To have a lawful society involves the total
structure of our society . . . faith in ourselves
. . . faith in our institutions . . . our political and
economic system and yes, faith and confidence
that the American dream of liberty and justice
for all still burns fiercely within all our hearts.

Speech
Oct. 29, 1972

LEADERSHIP

The most essential ingredient for America's future prosperity has less to do with productivity and our trade balance than it does with the larger issue of how America sees itself and its role in the world.

We did not seek the role of leadership that has been thrust upon us. But whether we like it or not, the events of our time demand America's participation.

Speech
Oct. 12, 1972

LIBERTY

Individual liberty depends upon keeping government under control.

Interview
Dec. 30, 1974

LOTTERY

Right now in Sacramento they are talking about a lottery. They say it will raise several hundred millions of dollars. But you never heard anyone say "Lets have a lottery to raise two hundred million dollars and then lets cut the people's taxes by two hundred million dollars. "The lottery is just more money for more government spending.

Interview
Feb. 7, 1974

The Quotable
Ronald Reagan

MARIJUANA

Some of the same people who favor banning the advertising of tobacco on television want to legalize the smoking of marijuana.

Speech
May 22, 1972

MARRIAGE

When I was first Governor it seemed like every day brought more and more problems but one day I was on the way to the office when I heard a disc jockey who became a great favorite of mine. Out of the clear blue sky he said, "Everybody should take unto himself a wife, because sooner or later something is bound to happen you can't blame on the Governor."

Speech
August 9, 1973

McGOVERN

Senator McGovern has made enough speeches on enough issues for most Americans to realize that whatever it is he stands for, it is not what most Americans want for their country.

Speech
Sept. 30, 1972

MENTAL ILLNESS

We have people coming to California from every state in the union because of the progress we have made in the treatment of the mentally ill. A few years ago, all over the world, mentally ill were put in what were called hospitals but were really warehouses. There was no effort made to cure them and get them back into society. We now have reduced the population in our mental hospitals from over 27,000 to only 7,000.

Students
March 8, 1973

MONOPOLY

A great many people today who call themselves liberals are not against monopoly if it is government or labor monopoly. Well, I think monopoly is wrong, not just who is doing it.

Interview
Sept. 15, 1973

MORAL LAW

I think there is a basic moral law. I don't think there is anything wrong with teaching a small child who is in kindergarten, if he wants the toy that the other child has, he doesn't bop him on the head to get it. I think you teach them the rights of others.

If you refuse to have any consideration for any moral standards or guidelines, you are in effect, saying, "There are none." But this can be done [the teaching of the differences between right and wrong] without teaching someone your particular philosophy, or teaching someone a religious creed.

Students
Feb. 13, 1973

The Quotable
Ronald Reagan

NARCOTICS

Drugs are not a fad or a phase to be compared to flagpole sitting or goldfish swallowing. The use of hard narcotics is largely responsible for the increase in burglaries, muggings and many of the irrational violent crimes in recent years.

Speech
Feb. 11, 1974

NATIONAL DEFENSE

National Defense is not a threat to peace; it is the guarantee of peace with freedom.

Speech
June 22, 1972

NUCLEAR POWER

There is almost a superstitious fear of what could happen in an accident to a nuclear power plant. Yet we don't have any background to justify these fears. In Sweden, they have built an atomic power plant under one of their cities.

Students
April 12, 1973

NUTS

California produces 40 percent of America's fresh fruits, vegetables and nuts—the kind you eat. We have had a bumper crop of the other variety too . . . the kind who would have us turn back the clock, forget about developing and maintaining the water supply we need for crops, for people and for industries.

Speech
April 27, 1973

The Quotable
Ronald Reagan

OFFICIALS

There is only one way to make government bite the bullet on inflation, on high taxes, on all those things that should be a matter of concern. And that is to hold all elected officials accountable. Match their performance with their promises, and if you find some who don't measure up, vote them out of office.

Speech
Oct. 15, 1974

ORANGES

Those who like to say California is a good place to be if you are an orange will be delighted, I'm sure, to know that now we have more acres in almonds than we do in oranges.

Speech
Dec. 11, 1972

The Quotable
Ronald Reagan

PEACE

We all share the love of peace, but our sons and daughters must learn two lessons men every-where and in every time have had to learn; that the price of freedom is dear but not nearly so costly as the loss of freedom—and that the advance and continuation of civilization depend on those values for which men have always been willing to die.

Speech
June 22, 1972

PEACE

The dust-bin of history is littered with the remains of those countries which relied on diplomacy to secure their freedom. We must never forget . . . in the final analysis . . . that it is our military, industrial and economic strength that offers the best guarantee of peace for America in times of danger.

Speech
Sept. 9, 1974

PEACE

Every lesson of history tells us that appeasement does not lead to peace. It invites an aggressor to test the will of a nation unprepared to meet that test. And tragically, those who seemingly want peace the most, our young people, pay the heaviest price for our failure to maintain our strength.

Speech
Sept. 15, 1972

PEACENIKS

Teddy Roosevelt said America should walk softly and carry a big stick. I don't think he had in mind those characters who walk barefoot and carry a peace symbol on their way to throw rocks at a policeman.

Speech
Sept. 15, 1972

PERMISSIVENESS

The virus of permissiveness spreads its deadly
poison. There are constant efforts to excuse, to
explain and ultimately, I suppose, to accept
widespread drug addiction as inevitable. I reject
this theory of inevitability.

Speech
Feb. 11, 1974

PERMISSIVENESS

If logic could muster a majority in our legisla-
tures and our courts, we would have no diffi-
culty reaffirming the moral standards that
helped shape America. The permissive
philosophy cannot stand up to the test of logic.

Speech
May 22, 1972

POISE

I have learned that one of the most important rules in politics is poise—which means looking like an owl after you have behaved like a jackass.

Speech
Aug. 9, 1973

POLITICIANS

The people who hold public office today are no better, no worse than the people that send them to public office and you cannot expect them to be. They are representative of you.

Students
June 21, 1973

POLITICIANS

I was a little disappointed that in about three weeks after I was elected, I had automatically in some people's minds become a politician. I still don't think about myself as such.

Students
June 21, 1973

POLITICIANS

Let me tell you what I have learned from looking at those elected to office from the inside. For every one that's bad, for everyone that can be bought, I will tell you there are scores who have never done a favor on the basis of someone's help in getting them elected or on the basis of a campaign contribution. As a matter of fact, I can tell you on behalf of those who contribute to political campaigns, no one has ever come to me in the years I have been Governor and sought a favor or special privilege on the basis of campaign aid or something he might have done to help me achieve this office, not one.

Students
June 21, 1973

POLITICIANS

One thing our founding fathers could not foresee . . . they were farmers, professional men, businessmen giving of their time and effort to a dream and an idea that became a country . . . was a nation governed by professional politicians who had a vested interest in getting reelected. They probably envisioned a fellow serving a couple of hitches and then looking eagerly forward to getting back to the farm.

Interview
Sept. 15, 1973

POLITICIANS

The reason there is a cynical lack of confidence in government is because too many politicians are elected to office but never try to carry out their campaign promises.

Speech
Oct. 15, 1974

POLLUTION

For more than thirty years government has been monitoring air in 52 of the largest cities in the United States. By and large, the air is purer in spite of smog. You see, when you talk about air pollutants, you can't just say "smog." You have what they call particulates, dirt that has been kicked up, and so forth. All of these things . . .

Once upon a time, within my lifetime, all of the houses on cold mornings had a chimney that was belching coal smoke from coal furnaces. Once you didn't have that automobile smog, but you had those chimneys. And you had wood stoves, cooking stoves in the kitchen where now you have gas and electric ranges. So don't think that the world is being destroyed before you get there. It's actually improving, and actually quite a bit. Take it from someone who goes quite a ways back.

Students
March 22, 1973

POLLUTION

You cannot live and be a human being without polluting the air . . . we are polluting it every time we take a breath in this room. So some place along the line we must set a realistic standard.

Speech
March 7, 1973

POLLUTION

We must control pollution and preserve the best of our environment in a way that is compatible with the goals and philosophy of a free society.

Speech
April 7, 1972

POLLUTION

"We have tried to apply common sense to our pollution problems. I have said before, there are three kinds of pollution today; real, hysterical and political.

To listen to some, you would think we will soon be standing shoulder to shoulder in the tiny center parkway of a giant freeway.

You could take the entire population of the United States and put it in the land area of only two states—California and Texas—and you could still have a population density lower than that of most of Western Europe.

Now, this does not mean we should not be concerned about the environment or that we can go on with practices that led to pollution —the real kind.

Speech
April 27, 1973

POLLUTION

The ultimate answer to air pollution is through technology. And that answer is far more likely to come from the engineers in the factories, not from the economists in Washington.

Speech
Nov. 12, 1973

PORNOGRAPHY

Some of the so-called experts vehemently declare that violence on television is bad, but turn around and claim pornography has no impact whatsoever on our young people.

Speech
Feb. 11, 1974

PORNOGRAPHY

Some of the obscenity freely available is so offensive, so far beyond the moral standard of the society, that laymen have no trouble recognizing it for what it is . . . simple, hardcore pornography, produced and sold for profit.

Speech
Oct. 29, 1972

POVERTY

When I was a boy 90% of the people in this country lived below what today we consider the poverty line. Two-thirds of the people of the United States at the time of my birth lived in what is called substandard housing. Today, it's only 10%.

Students
March 8, 1973

POVERTY

Not quite a decade ago, government declared war on poverty . . . poverty won.

Speech
Oct. 29, 1972

PRECEDENCE

Putting our economic house in order is America's greatest imperative and it must take precedence over everything else.

Speech
Oct. 15, 1974

PREJUDICE

My generation has come a long way in ending bigotry and prejudice. It didn't end it of course, there are always going to be people who have prejudice in their hearts.

Students
April 12, 1973

PRIVATE ENTERPRISE

Eighty percent of the jobs in this country are in the private sector and it is from the private sector, from business, industry and from individuals, that government receives its operating funds.

Speech
May 30, 1973

PROFESSIONALS

Government is too important to be left to those who are not too busy—the professionals who think government has some sort of divine right to tell people what is good for them.

Speech
Oct. 29, 1972

PROFIT

Today in many people's minds, profit is a dirty word. Profit is the legitimate earnings that someone gets on his investment. The average citizen should understand it if he has a savings account. The bank pays him for the privilege of using his money.

A poll recently showed that people believed companies are making a 28% profit. The after-tax profit on business in the United States runs less than 5%.

Interview
Feb. 7, 1974

PROPERTY TAX

The property tax is an antiquated tax. It came into existence before income taxes and was a kind of an income tax when most of the revenues came from the land.

Students
April 12, 1973

PROGRESS

The key to progress is not a federal subsidy or another government program. The true secret of America's greatness is freedom, the dynamic working together of millions of individuals, each seeking an individual goal in a society that assures them the freedom to climb as high as their own drive, ambition and talent can take them.

Speech
Nov. 14, 1974

PROSPERITY

I believe expanded commercial contacts can do more to stimulate peace and prosperity than any other single development. It can generate greater understanding among the people of the world and it can provide a growing prosperity for everyone.

Speech
May 22, 1974

POPULATION

You could take the entire population of the United States and put it into the land area of only two states—California and Texas—and you would still have a population density lower than that of most of Western Europe.

Speech
April 27, 1973

The Quotable
Ronald Reagan

RAPID TRANSIT

Everybody driving on the freeway in the rush hour is looking at the traffic and saying "we should have rapid transit because if we did, all those people would be riding it and I would have the freeway to myself."

Students
April 12, 1975

REGULATIONS

Those who advocate more and more government regulation have been experimenting for 40 years, trying to create an economic system in which everyone can somehow be made more prosperous by the toil of someone else.

Speech
Oct. 15, 1974

RESEARCH

A senate committee set up a distinguished re-
search team, headed by a prestigious professor,
who discovered that if you cut bus fares in half,
more people would ride the bus. They got so
excited about their discovery, they pursued it
and learned you can further increase patronage
if you pay people a dime to ride the bus. And
even more people will ride if you pay them 20
cents. But then they had to report failure. They
discovered that even when you pay people you
cannot get 100 per cent use of rapid transit. This
is my kind of sneaky way of telling that 60 million Americans still drive to work each day and
we will be supporting new highways for years to
come.

Speech
Sept. 8, 1972

RESOURCES

We know we can no longer tolerate the philosophy of deplete and be damned—because quite simply, our natural resources constitute the single greatest asset we have to improve not only the quality of our own lives, but the lives of the generations which will follow us.

Speech
April 7, 1972

RESPONSIBILITY

There is no way for America to turn inward and embrace isolationism in the world as it is today without jeopardizing all the progress we have made toward peace in this century. For those genuinely concerned with peace and willing to pay the price for it, there is only one path to choose. It is not the easiest; it is the wisest. If we carry the burden of responsibility destiny has placed on our shoulders, we do not become a drop-out in world affairs.

Speech
Oct. 12, 1972

RESPONSIBILITY

We derive our ultimate authority from the people. And we have an obligation to make sure that in carrying out our responsibilities, we do so at a price they can afford.

Speech
Oct. 24, 1973

REVENUE

Government does not produce revenue. It consumes it.

Speech
Nov. 14, 1974

REVOLUTIONARIES

No amount of rhetoric can change a crime into a social or political cause. Kidnapping is a violent crime and those who engage in this kind of terrorism, whatever their alleged motives, are not romantic revolutionaries; they are common, sordid, vicious criminals and should be treated accordingly.

Speech
May 2, 1974

RULERS

Americans do not want to be part of a political philosophy that views the individual as part of some voting bloc. They do not want to be ruled by government. They want to be represented in a government ruled by the people.

Speech
Feb. 3, 1973

The Quotable
Ronald Reagan

SCHOOL

Your teachers will hate me for this but my favorite subject in college was football. Today, I am fascinated with history.

Students
March 8, 1973

SECOND RATE

Reducing America to the status of a second class nation, unable to make its voice heard in the councils of the world will surely be the prelude to another generation of Americans dying needlessly because of our mistakes.

Speech
Sept. 15, 1972

SELFISHNESS

The world as we have known it in the quarter century after World War II is undergoing some profound changes. Will we react to these changes in our world as a people divided and distrustful of each other, pursuing selfish interests no matter what the cost to others or to the ultimate good of our country?

Speech
Feb. 15, 1972

SMALL BUSINESSMEN

Small businessmen in America spend 130 million man hours a year just filling out government forms. That blizzard of paperwork adds $30 to 50 billion a year to the cost of doing business and it means higher prices on the products you buy.

Speech
Nov. 14, 1974

SMOG

It will not do anyone much good to have a smogless car if there are no roads to drive on or if they cannot get enough fuel to drive, either because of a shortage or because it has become too expensive to operate a car.

Speech
Nov. 17, 1972

SOCIETY

Right now, America is caught between two whirlwinds forcing potentially massive disruptions in our society, the effort to protect the environment and the world wide energy shortage.

Speech
Nov. 17, 1972

SPENDING

Ask any citizen on any day if taxes are too high, if government spends too much, and if he would like to have a say about government's right to confiscate his earnings. The answer would be, "hell yes!"

Speech
Sept. 7, 1973

SPENDING

When a business or an individual spends more than it makes, it goes bankrupt. When government does, it sends you—the taxpayer—the bill.

Speech
Oct. 15, 1974

SST

Of all the planes flying commercially in the world, 85 percent bear an American trademark and were made by American working men. We captured this market because we were out in front with every new development. When planes became bigger, we built them first. When they became faster we were first with the fastest . . . until we reached the sound barrier. Then little men with little minds voted no on the SST. In reality, they were voting to give up America's supremacy in the sky.

Speech
Sept. 5, 1972

STATESMEN

Harry Truman once said a statesman is what they call a politician after he is safely dead. At this moment in our history, what we need is more live statesmen—at every level of public life. Government's only reason for existing is to serve the people. If we are to serve their needs, we must cast politics aside. We must demonstrate that government deserves the public's trust.

Speech
Jan. 9, 1974

STRIKES

I believe in collective bargaining in the private sector. I do not believe in it for the public sector because I do not believe that public employees can be allowed to strike. Public employees are striking against the people and the people are the highest source of power other than the Lord Himself that the government has.

Students
April 12, 1973

SUBSIDY

This old fellow bought some corn, loaded into his wagon and started off down the road to the town swamp. He told his neighbors he was going to catch the wild pigs in the swamp. Well, those pigs had been there for fifty years and nobody had ever caught them so his friends thought he had gone looney. Well, it wasn't many weeks before he came back to town and he had the pigs.

How did he do it? Well, he began putting corn out and gradually he bult a fence in back of the corn. Pretty soon, he extended it onto two sides and by this time, the pigs were eating together. He finally put the final side in and soon had the pigs eating out of his hand . . . and he owned them.

Well once government starts giving handouts and you take them, they own you and that is what has happened to the fourth of farmers in the U.S. who have been subsidized.

Interview
Sept. 8, 1973

SUPPLY & DEMAND

No one has yet found a way to repeal the law of supply and demand.

Speech
Nov. 17, 1972

SQUIRRELS

In Sacramento, some very kind hearted people concerned about the squirrels in the capitol grounds—decided to do something about it. For years, one of the legislators has been buying nuts to make sure they have enough to eat. He passed away, so another legislator recently took up the task. The first day he went out with the walnuts, he had trouble getting them to eat. Then one of the bystanders said, "you have to crack them first." He did and had the squirrels eating out of his hands.

America has the resources, the skills and the experience to meet all our needs, to feed and clothe our people, to maintain our prosperity, to meet whatever challenges we might face in the future.

But if we expect to do it, we cannot become too dependent on government or anyone else. We cannot be like those squirrels. We have got to crack a few walnuts ourselves.

Speech
Dec. 14, 1973

The Quotable
Ronald Reagan

TAXES

It's easy to say to the people, "We are going to relieve you of the tax burden and we are going to make business pay more of the share." But everytime a tax is assessed on business, it becomes buried in the price structure. This does not mean business is hiding anything but every cost of production, rent, cost of labor, fuel, etc. must be included in the price of the product or the businessman cannot stay in business. Therefore you come back to the old rule that only people pay taxes.

Interview
Feb. 7, 1974

TAXES

There are by actual count one hundred sixteen taxes on a suit of clothes. There are one hundred and fifty one in a loaf of bread.

Interview
Feb. 7, 1974

TAXES

The typical citizen works almost six months of the year to pay his per capita share of the total tax burden.

Speech
April 30, 1973

TAXES

History reveals that no society has long survived a tax burden that reached one-third of the people's earnings. Looking back on the fallen empires of the past, one sees the first warning signs appear. As the burden grows heavier, there is a growing lack of respect for government and the law. Fraud becomes widespread and crime increases. Are we to say none of those things is taking place here.

Speech
May 23, 1973

TAXES

If we continue to saddle our people and the private sector with a tax burden that takes half or more of their income, there will come a day when the free economic system that generates all taxes will be simply unable to carry the load.

Speech
May 29, 1973

TAXES

No country in history has ever long survived a tax burden that reached one third of its citizens' earnings. Indeed, the first signs of disintegration begin when the total tax burden hits 25 percent.

Speech
May 30, 1973

TAXES

I am sure I will get no argument if I say the cost of living is too high. I *am* getting an argument, however, for saying taxes are too high, that the best thing government can do to fight inflation is to let the people keep more of their own money. Reducing the percentage that government takes out of the private sector is the best service government can perform for the people.

Speech
Aug. 6, 1973

TAXES

It is a funny thing: no one ever threw rocks at us for proposing to spend more money. But there was a constant volley from every direction every time we tried to keep the budget in line, to hold down taxes so our people would have more of their own money to keep for themselves.

Speech
Sept. 21, 1973

TAXES

If the historic trend of the last few decades continues uninterrupted, in 15 years, government will be taking 67 percent of personal income—if a free economy can survive a tax burden that tops two thirds of the people's earnings.

Speech
Oct. 19, 1973

TELEVISION

The experts who keep up with these things say that by the time a typical American youngster finishes high school, he has watched about 22,000 hours of television—twice the time he has spent in the classroom . . . To some of our young people, Granny Goose is better known than Mother Goose.

Speech
March 3, 1972

TELEVISION

Because TV is the type of medium it is, bias cannot always be measured solely in the amount of time given to one side or the other . . . or to explanations of what is missing from the film story. The inflection of the announcer's voice . . . the arched eyebrow . . . the skeptical expression . . . and those can and have injected an element of bias in television news.

Speech
May 4 1972

TELEVISION ANALYSTS

You sit there and you watch your television set, and you hear a man make a speech to you. And they switch off, and three men or four men, or one man sits there and says, "I will now tell you what he said for the last thirty minutes." Frankly, I've always found it a little insulting to my intelligence. You just heard the man. I don't need someone to put it all together and say, "Now, here's what he really said."

Students
Oct. 15, 1973

THIRD TERM

I think the two terms is enough for a Governor. I think there is a risk that a man who wanted to set up a political machine has a better opportunity to do that . . . in the Governor's Office.

Rocklin School
March 8, 1973

TRADE

Constructive trade, the two-way exchange of goods and services, is the most efficient and logical way for each nation and each area of the world to build a stable prosperity, a prosperity based not on aid, but on mutually beneficial economic contacts.

Speech
May 22, 1974

TREATIES

There was a time in the not too distant past when you could have taken all the non-aggression pacts and disarmament treaties with their beribboned seals and signatures and papered the walls of the League of Nations.

If that is too cynical a view, let me "make it perfectly clear," that along with a willingness to negotiate, America can best protect the peace by maintaining a realistic and credible ability to defend itself should the need occur.

Speech
Oct. 12, 1972

The Quotable
Ronald Reagan

UNEMPLOYED

They were going to put seventeen unemployed people to work in a so-called training project clearing some park land. I vetoed the program because they were going to spend half the budget on seven administrators to see that the seventeen got to work on time.

Students
April 12, 1973

UNITY

Americans want a united country, not one divided into ethnic, religious, and economic groupings.

Speech
Feb. 15, 1972

The Quotable
Ronald Reagan

VALUES

Whenever America has faced a crisis, we somehow always produce the leaders and the men needed to carry us through to victory. That is part of the strength of our system. It cannot be explained with the logical precision of a computer program. Perhaps that is because spiritual values can never be adequately measured in material terms. Things like faith, love of country, courage and dedication—they are all part of the inner strength of America. And sometimes, they do not become self-evident until there is a time of crisis.

Speech
Sept. 9, 1974

VIETNAM

There is a lesson in the Vietnam war for all of us. If military power must be exerted to preserve our freedom or that of our allies, the purpose must be clearly spelled out for the people . . . before the first troops go ashore.

Speech
Sept. 9, 1974

VIETNAM

Our reason for being here today is to dedicate a memorial to the 6,000 Californians who gave their lives in the defense of freedom in Southeast Asia.

There are those who say that Vietnam was a war without heroes, because the conflict became a controversy that divided our people for so long. I do not accept that. They were all heroes, expecially those we are honoring here today.

Speech
Feb. 11, 1974

VIETNAM

Never again must this country ask a young man to fight and die unless it is for something we believe in so much that we tell him at the same time "we're going to turn our full energies behind you to get it over with and to win it."

Students
April 26, 1973

VOLUNTEERS

The work of volunteer groups throughout our country represent the very heart and soul of America. They have helped make this the most compassionate, generous and humane society that ever existed on the face of this earth.

Speech
Oct. 16, 1973

The Quotable
Ronald Reagan

WAR

Armaments do not cause war. Armaments are built and used by aggressors whose intentions from the beginning is war and the threat of war. Peace loving nations must match their weaponry whether they like it or not or fall victim to their aggressor.

Speech
June 22, 1972

WAR

All of us denounce war—all of us consider it man's greatest stupidity. And yet wars happen and they involve the most passionate lovers of peace because there are still barbarians in the world who set the price for peace at death or enslavement and the price is too high.

Speech
Sept. 15, 1972

WEAPONS

From the beginning of time man has deplored the need for weapons. A sword is not as productive as a plowshare. But over this same span of years, men have learned to their sorrow you have to have both sword and plowshare or you must one day choose between slavery and death.

Speech
Sept. 5, 1972

WELFARE

Welfare should help the blind, disabled, the aged who cannot provide for themselves. The other people on welfare . . . the able-bodied . . . would be treated as people temporarily out of work. The rest of us have to help them out until we can get them back to work again and that is the principle of welfare as I see it.

Students
March 3, 1973

WELFARE

Welfare's excesses are like a double-jointed oc-
topus with remarkable regenerative powers.
When you wriggle free of one tentacle, another
grows in its place and squeezes the public's
purse strings a little tighter.

Speech
Aug. 9, 1974

WOMEN'S LIBERATION

I've never really felt the need of women's lib.
I've always thought that you were in charge of
things, and I've never squawked about it, I kind
of like it that way.

Students
Sept. 24, 1973